D0990815

France

Helen Arnold

RSVP
RAINTREE
STECK-VAUGHN
PUBLISHERS
The Steck-Vaughn Company

Austin, Texas

© Copyright 1996 text Steck-Vaughn Company

All rights reserved. No part of this book may be reproduced or utilized in any form or by any means, electronic or mechanical, including photocopying, recording, or by any information storage and retrieval system, without permission in writing from the Publisher. Inquiries should be addressed to: Copyright Permissions, Steck-Vaughn Company, P.O. Box 26015, Austin, TX 78755.

Published by Raintree Steck-Vaughn Publishers, an imprint of Steck-Vaughn Company

A ZOË BOOK

Editor: Kath Davies, Helene Resky
Design: Jan Sterling, Sterling Associates
Map: Gecko Limited
Production: Grahame Griffiths

Library of Congress Cataloging-in-Publication Data

Arnold, Helen.
    France / Helen Arnold.
        p. cm. — (Postcards from)
    Includes index.
    ISBN 0-8172-4004-7 (lib. binding)
    ISBN 0-8172-4225-2 (softcover)
    1. France — Description and travel — Juvenile literature.
    2. Postcards — France — Juvenile Literature. I. Title. II. Series.
    DC20.2.A76 1996
    944–dc20   95–10118
                                                                     CIP

Printed and bound in the United States
    2 3 4 5 6 7 8 9 0 WZ 99 98 97

Photographic acknowledgments

The publishers wish to acknowledge, with thanks, the following photographic sources:

The Hutchison Library / Tony Souter - cover bl, 6; / Gail Goodger 14; / Bernard Regent 16, 24; / J.G. Fuller 18; / Pierrette Collomb 28; Robert Harding Picture Library 20, 22; Impact Photos / Ray Roberts - title page; / Buthaud/Cosmos 12; Zefa - cover tl & r, 8, 10, 26.

The publishers have made every effort to trace the copyright holders, but if they have inadvertently overlooked any, they will be pleased to make the necessary arrangement at the first opportunity.

Contents

All the words that appear in **bold** are explained in the Glossary on page 30.

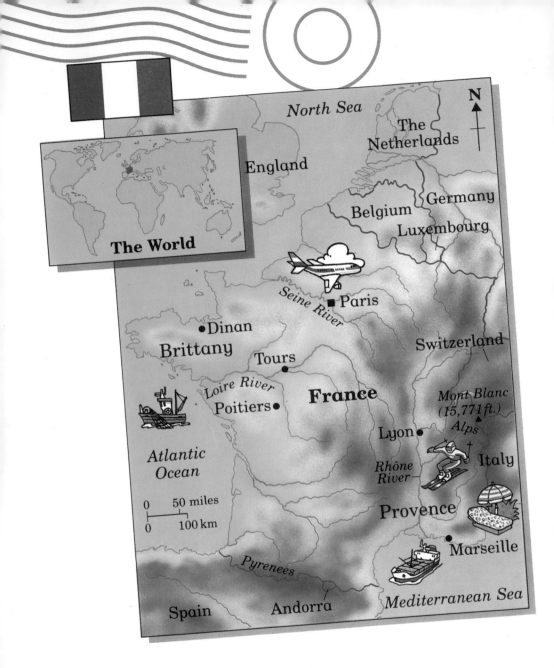

The World

A big map of France
and a small map of the world

Dear Marie,

We are in your country now!
The plane from Houston took
about nine hours to fly to Paris.
We flew across the Atlantic
Ocean to Europe to get there.

Love,

Tamara

P.S. Our teacher says that France is much
smaller than the United States. About five
times more people live in the United States
than in France.

The Eiffel Tower, Paris

Dear Tom,

We took three elevators to get to the top of the Eiffel Tower. It is about 985 feet (300 m) high. It is in Paris, which is the **capital** city of France. We had a great view of the city from the top of the tower.

Your friend,

Will

P.S. Mom says that Paris is one of the biggest cities in Europe. Paris is full of traffic. We go on the **subway**, which is called the Metro.

The Seine River and Notre Dame Cathedral, Paris

Dear Melanie,

We took a trip on a boat like this one. The Seine River flows through the middle of Paris. We could see many old buildings from the boat. I liked the **cathedral** best.

Au revoir

(that means "Good-bye"),

Ruth

P.S. Quite a few people in Paris speak some English. People speak French though most of the time.

A food store in Dinan, Brittany

Dear Roy,

The food in France is great! Dad gives us French money called *francs*. We buy long sticks of fresh bread every morning. Sometimes we buy snacks as well. I like apple pie best.

Your friend,

Andy

P.S. There are different stores for each kind of food in France. One store sells cakes, and another store sells bread.

The TGV *Atlantique* at Tours station

Dear Phil,

The French high-speed train is called the TGV. It is one of the fastest trains in the world. It can travel at 180 miles an hour (290 kph). We are going to Tours on this train.

Your brother,

Shane

P.S. Dad says that France is so big that the best way to travel is by train. The trains are clean and fast. They always arrive on time!

A street market in Provence,
southern France

Dear Jessie,

Every small town has a street market. This one is in Vence. Farmers bring their fresh **produce** to the market. They grow all kinds of fruits and vegetables. We bought some juicy peaches today.

Love,

Fran

P.S. Mom says that the French people make more than 365 kinds of cheese. We could eat a different cheese each day for a year!

Lyon, on the Rhône River

Dear Luke,

Lyon is one of the largest cities in France. Many people here live in **high-rise** apartments. Lyon is toward the south of France, on the banks of the Rhône River.

Yours,

Gavin

P.S. Uncle Jim says that some of the boats, called **barges**, on the Rhône River come from Germany. They take heavy **goods** south to Marseille on the Mediterranean Sea.

17

A beach on the French Riviera,
in the south of France

Dear Jan,

At last we are at the beach!
I have been swimming a lot.
The Mediterranean Sea is very
warm. This coast is called the
Riviera. It has many famous
beaches and towns. Movie
stars come here to vacation.

Love,

Inga

P.S. Mom says that families from all over
Europe come here for their summer vacations.
That is why the beaches are so crowded.

A skiing school in the French Alps

Dear Jake,

French children have a one-week vacation in the spring to go skiing. This skiing school is near the highest mountain in the Alps. The mountain is called Mont Blanc, which means "White Mountain."

See you soon,

Raoul

P.S. Mom says that French children have a longer school day than ours. They work very hard at school and get lots of homework.

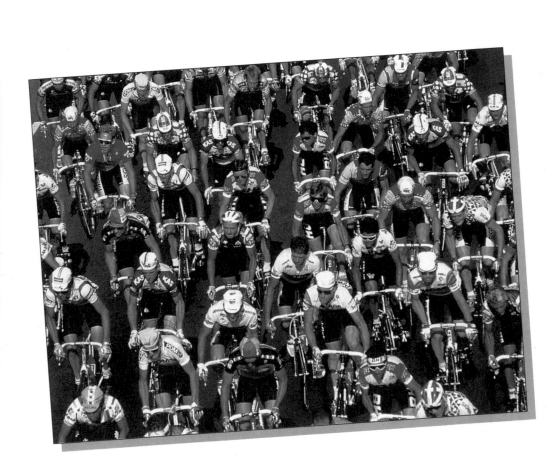

Bicyclists in the Tour de France race

Dear Sandy,

The French are good at many sports. This bicycle race is one of the most famous in the world. It is held each year, and it lasts for three weeks. The bicyclists ride about 2,000 miles (3,220 km) mostly through France.

Love,

Mimi

P.S. Dad says that at the end of each day of bicycling the leader is given a yellow shirt to wear the next day.

The Futuroscope park near Poitiers

Dear Terry,

Futuroscope is a wonderful **amusement park**. We spent the whole day here, but we did not see everything. You can see some of the space-age buildings in the picture.

Love,

Debra

P.S. Mom says that many children in France go to college when they leave school. Some of them come to the college at Futuroscope. They learn about new **technology**.

The *château* of Chenonceaux in the Loire valley

Dear Mel,

The French word for a big house or a castle is a *château*. We went on a trip to the Loire valley to see some of these houses. I liked this one best. It is on the banks of the Loire River.

Yours,

Tom

P.S. Mom says that some rich French **nobles** built *châteaux* in the Loire valley more than 300 years ago. It only took them a day to get here from Paris by coach.

French flags

Dear Gina,

The French flag is called the *tricolore,* which means "three colors" in French. This flag was first flown about 200 years ago. The red and blue come from the flag for Paris. The white is from the king's flag.

Love,

Shelley

P.S. Aunt Terese says that during the French **revolution**, the king was killed. France became a **republic**. Today French people choose their own leaders. France is a **democracy**.

Glossary

Amusement park: A park that has rides and stands, where food and drinks are sold

Barge: A long boat that has a flat bottom. Barges are used to carry heavy goods.

Capital: The town or city where people who rule the country meet. It is not always the biggest city in the country.

Cathedral: The most important Christian church in an area. The leader of the group of churches in an area is called a bishop.

Democracy: A country where all the people choose the leaders they want to run the country

Goods: Things that can be sold

High-rise: Having many floors

Noble: A person who has been given a title such as "Lord" or "Lady" by the king or queen. The title passes from the parent to the child, when the parent dies.

Produce: Food that is grown or made, such as fruit, cheese, eggs, and milk

P.S.: This stands for Post Script. A postscript is the part of a card or letter that is added at the end, after the person has signed it.

Republic: A country where the people choose their leaders. A republic does not have a king or queen.

Revolution: A complete change in the way a country is ruled

Subway: A train that runs under the ground

Technology: the study of ways of using science to help people to do things or to make goods

Index

© 1995 Zoë Books Limited